RECORD BREAKERS
MOTO X

Blaine Wiseman

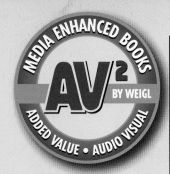

BOOK CODE

C 7 7 8 1 9 6

AV² **by Weigl** brings you media enhanced books that support active learning.

AV² provides enriched content that supplements and complements this book. Weigl's AV² books strive to create inspired learning and engage young minds for a total learning experience.

Go to **www.av2books.com**, and enter this book's unique code. You will have access to video, audio, web links, quizzes, a slide show, and activities.

Audio
Listen to sections of the book read aloud.

Video
Watch informative video clips.

Web Link
Find research sites and play interactive games.

Try This!
Complete activities and hands-on experiments.

Due to the dynamic nature of the Internet, some of the URLs and activities provided as part of AV² by Weigl may have changed or ceased to exist. AV² by Weigl accepts no responsibility for any such changes. All media enhanced books are regularly monitored to update addresses and sites in a timely manner. Contact AV² by Weigl at 1-866-649-3445 or av2books@weigl.com with any questions, comments, or feedback.

Published by AV² by Weigl
350 5th Avenue, 59th Floor
New York, NY 10118
Website: www.av2books.com   www.weigl.com

Library of Congress Cataloging-in-Publication Data available upon request.
Fax 1-866-44-WEIGL for the attention of the Publishing Records department.

ISBN 978-1-61690-115-8 (hard cover)
ISBN 978-1-61690-116-5 (soft cover)

Printed in the United States of America in North Mankato, Minnesota
1 2 3 4 5 6 7 8 9 0 14 13 12 11 10

052010
WEP264000

Project Coordinator Heather C. Hudak
Design Terry Paulhus

Contents

High Flyers

Robbie Maddison

Lift-off in Las Vegas

Robbie Maddison has become one of the best-known motocross, or moto X, daredevils. Maddison celebrated the New Year in 2009 by performing a spectacular stunt in Las Vegas. "Maddo" rode to the top of a ramp and jumped onto the **Arc de Triomphe** at the Paris Las Vegas hotel. The Arc de Triomphe stands 96 feet high, but Maddo had to jump 120 feet (36.6 meters) total to clear the landing. He then drove off the edge of the Arc de Triomphe and landed on another ramp, dropping more than 50 feet (15.2 m) straight down.

Biker Girls

Jolene Van Vugt

In recent years, moto X has become popular with female riders. Women riders, such as Jolene Van Vugt, are breaking many records and finding success as professionals in the sport. Van Vugt was the first woman to complete a backflip on a motorbike. In 2006, she set a record for the longest backflip by a female rider, at 60 feet (18.3 m). The following year, Van Vugt became the first female to backflip her bike into the Grand Canyon.

Road Renner

In order to break records, moto X riders perform extreme stunts. Ronnie Renner set the world record for highest jump out of a **quarter pipe** in July 2008. He jumped an incredible 59 feet 2 inches (18 m) into the air and came straight back down. A year later, in July 2009, Renner broke his own record. In front of thousands of fans in Chicago, he soared 63 feet 5 inches (19.3 m) above the ground.

Ronnie Renner

Wonderboy

A well-known motocross X athlete is Travis "Wonderboy" Pastrana. Pastrana is a legend of action sports, setting records driving dirt bikes, all terrain vehicles (ATVs), and rally cars. Pastrana has parachuted off his motorcycle into the Grand Canyon and jumped out of an airplane without a parachute. At the **X Games** in 2006, Pastrana became the first person to complete a double backflip on a motorcycle. It was the most daring motocross trick ever caught on camera. Here are some of Pastrana's records.

Most motorcycle backflips in 30 seconds – 8
Longest **tandem** motorcycle backflip – 16 feet 5 inches (5 m)
Lowest motorcycle backflip – 3 feet (0.9 m)

Travis Pastrana

Long Jumpers

Making a Scene

Moto X riders have made history by becoming the first to perform stunts at certain monuments around the world. Athletes do tricks at these specials sites in order to draw attention to the sport. Robbie Maddison's New Year's Eve jumps took place at well-known hotels on the Las Vegas Strip. In addition to his stunts on U.S. soil, Maddison is the only moto X rider to complete a trick on the Tower Bridge in London, England. Maddison did a backflip 72 feet (22 m) above the Thames River, flipping across the open drawbridge.

Robbie Maddison

Evel Knievel

In 1968, Evel Knievel, the greatest legend in motorcycle stunting, crashed trying to jump over the fountains at Caesar's Palace in Las Vegas. In 2006, moto X rider Mike Metzger broke the world record for longest backflip on a motorcycle. He jumped 125 feet (38 m) over the same fountains Knievel had attempted to clear nearly 40 years earlier.

Mad Man

To celebrate the New Year in 2008, Robbie Maddison broke the world record for longest jump on a motorcycle. He leaped a distance of 322 feet 7.5 inches (98.4 m) at the Rio Hotel in Las Vegas. This is about the length of a football field. Maddison is always looking for new ways to push the limits.

Ryan Capes has jumped farther on a motorcycle than any other rider in history. In 2008, Ryan Capes flew 390 feet 4 inches (119 m) in Royal City, Washington. This is as far as the average home run in baseball. Capes hopes to become the first person to jump more than 400 feet (122 m) and prove that he is the greatest distance jumper in the world.

Trigger

Maddison's massive jump in 2008 broke the record set by motocross distance pioneer Trigger Gumm. In 2005, Gumm jumped 277 feet 6 inches (84.6 m) to break his own record. He has held the distance jumping record four times in his career. Gumm also holds the record for the highest jump, flying 80 feet (24.4 m) above the ground.

Robbie Maddison

Trigger Gumm

Speed Racers

Hear No Evil

Ashley Fiolek is a major force in women's motocross. In 2009, Fiolek won her first and second Women's Motocross Championships in a row. She also won her first X Games gold medal, finishing first in an exciting race that came down to the final lap. Fiolek is hearing impaired, so she relies on feel rather than sound to know when to change **gears** on her bike while she rides.

Ashley Fiolek

Long Ride

In 2009, Mark Savage rode his dirt bike for 24 hours so that he could raise money for charity. Savage completed 317 laps of the Jimboomba race course in Queensland, Australia. Money raised by the event helped kids with cancer and other local charities.

Adaptation

In 1995, moto X rider Chris Ridgway was in a crash that left his lower legs crushed. Several years later, his leg was **amputated**, and he began wearing a **prosthetic** leg. Within months, Ridgway had returned to riding his bike. Since then, he has broken records and won championships. Ridgway competes in adaptive moto X, a division for athletes with disabilities. The competition and skill level are extremely high. In 2008, adaptive moto X was included in the X Games, and Ridgway became the first amputee to win an X Games gold medal.

Chris Ridgway

The X Games

Medal Mayhem

The X Games is the biggest competition in the world of moto X. To win a medal, athletes must ride faster and jump higher than their competitors. Performing outrageous stunts also is a main feature of moto X competitions. Riders push the limits of their motorcycles to the extreme at the X Games. They often risk serious injury in each event. Travis Pastrana has won two bronze, four silver, and nine gold medals at the X Games.

Travis Pastrana

Jeremy Carter

Step It Up

A popular X Games moto X event is the Step Up competition. This event features a combination of high jumping and **freestyle** moto X. Riders launch themselves straight up into the air, trying to jump over a bar placed high above a ramp. The Step Up competition was first held in 2000, with Tommy Clowers jumping 35 feet (10.7 m) over the bar. Clowers won gold and set a record that still stands. In 2009, Ronnie Renner and Ricky Carmichael were both awarded gold medals in this event.

Golden Girls

Women's moto X became part of the X Games in 2008. The performances of the women at that event guaranteed that they would be part of all future X Games.

Tarah Gieger

2009
Gold – Ashley Fiolek
Silver – Jessica Patterson
Bronze – Elizabeth Bash

2008
Gold – Tarah Gieger
Silver – Sherri Cruse
Bronze – Tatum Sik

★ GOLD COLLECTORS ★

Five athletes have won two Winter X Games moto X gold medals. Brian Deegan, Tommy Clowers, Mike Metzger, Mike Jones, and Caleb Wyatt are tied for the record. Here are some other X Games Moto X records.

Jeremy Stenberg

Travis Pastrana
Most gold medals – 7 (two more in rally) – 1999–2009
Highest motocross freestyle score – 99.0 – 1999

Jeremy Stenberg and Nate Adams
Longest dirt-to-dirt backflip – 100 feet (30.48 m) – 2005

11

The Gear

The Bike

By adding new parts to their bikes, moto X riders can adjust the way they drive, fly, and land. Riders often adjust the speed of their bikes by adding new engines. **Suspension** helps the riders jump and land. Riders have a special way to tune their suspension. This is especially important to support the weight of the bike when landing huge, record-breaking jumps.

Marvin Musquin

Heads Up

Moto X riders fly through the air and crash to the ground on fast, powerful machines. With this kind of activity, many serious injuries can occur. For this reason, riders wear special equipment that protects them from injuries. A helmet is the most important piece of safety equipment in moto X. When riders crash to the ground, they can hit their head on the dirt or on the bike. A helmet can help prevent serious injuries. In 2001, Seth Enslow tried to break the world record for distance jumping. Enslow flew so far that he missed the landing ramp and landed on flat ground. The impact caused his head to hit the handle bars of the bike, cutting his forehead and breaking his skull. Enslow survived the crash, but he had a metal plate inserted into his forehead. Enslow's helmet saved his life.

Suit Up

Safety is the top concern for most moto X riders, especially when they are performing death-defying stunts. Riders wear protective equipment all over their bodies. Special gloves protect riders' hands, while boots keep their feet and ankles safe. Body armor covers the entire upper body, including the shoulders, chest, back, and arms. Special padded pants protect riders' legs. Many riders also wear a neck brace to protect against **whiplash**.

OLD TIMERS

The very first moto X motorcycles were regular bicycles with an engine attached. The specialized bicycles were used in the early part of the 20th century. The first moto X events were called "scrambles." People with motorized bikes would gather in **off-road** areas and race through the woods, up and down hills, and across creeks. The first scramble was held in Surrey, England, in 1924. Soon, tracks were built for moto X racing. Jumps were added to make events more challenging and exciting.

More Records

Crashed and Broken

Seth Enslow is better known for his 2001 crash than for breaking records. He was attempting to break the world record for distance but jumped too far. The video of Enslow's spectacular crash made him an instant celebrity. In another attempt to break the distance record in Las Vegas, Enslow jumped farther than any other rider in history. However, when he landed, his bike broke in two.

Seth Enslow

Envirocross

Moto X bikes have powerful engines that burn fuel to make them run. Burning fuel creates pollution. In recent years, companies have begun developing moto X bikes powered by electricity, which does not cause pollution. The first international electric motocross **endurance** race was held in 2009. Ten teams competed by riding their electric bikes for 24 hours, only stopping to change riders and batteries. The winning team, HotChalk, completed 1,015 laps of the course, riding more than 500 miles (800 kilometers). The team set a world record for distance traveled on an off-road motorcycle in 24 hours. The total amount of electricity used for all 10 bikes in the event cost only $100.

G.O.A.T.

Ricky Carmichael has earned the nickname "Greatest of All-time" (G.O.A.T.). Carmichael has won more American Motorcycle Association (AMA) moto X racing events than any other rider in history. He won seven moto X championships in a row and five supercross championships in six years. Carmichael was the first AMA rider to complete a perfect season, winning every race in 2002. He repeated this feat in 2004.

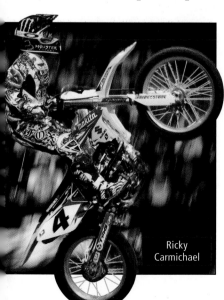

Ricky Carmichael

Hill Climbers

A popular type of moto X competition in the United States and Europe is called hill climbing. There are different types of hill climbing, but they all involve riders competing to reach the top of a hill in the shortest time. Glenn Curtiss won the very first hill climb in the United States in 1903. Curtiss, who later built airplanes, designed his own motorcycle.

The Pikes Peak International Hill Climb, also known as "The Race to the Clouds," is the best-known hill climbing competition in the United States. First held in 1916, the event showcases cars and motorcycles racing to the top of a 12.42-mile (19.99-km) course. The course is an uphill climb with 156 turns to the top of the mountain. Another well-known hill climbing event is the Bushkill Valley Hill Climb in Pennsylvania. At this event, riders try to reach the top of a steep hill. The rider who climbs the highest is the winner.

Records and Stunts

Moto X is popular all around the world. This map shows the places where some of the top moto X riders set a new record or became the first person to perform an extraordinary stunt.

Pacific Ocean

Ryan Capes
Farthest Jump
Reno, Nevada
390 feet, 4 inches (119 m)

Travis Pastrana
Double Backflip
Los Angeles, California

Mike Metzger
Longest Backflip
Las Vegas, Nevada
125 feet (38 m) over fountains at Caesar's Palace

N
W — E
S

210 Miles
0
338 Kilometers

Ronnie Renner

Highest Jump
Quarter Pipe
Chicago, Illinois
63 feet, 5 inches (19.3 m)

Atlantic Ocean

UNITED STATES

Mark Savage

Longest Time Riding

Jimboomba, Australia
He drove for 24 hours straight, completing 317 laps at the Jimboomba race course in Queensland, Australia.

AUSTRALIA

621 Miles

0   1,000 Kilometers

The Course

The Track

Moto X tracks offer many obstacles to challenge riders. During races, riders weave around corners and tight turns, flying through the air, barreling over **table tops**, bouncing on **whoops**, and climbing hills. Each type of obstacle tests riders in a different way. Record-breaking speed on these courses is often a recipe for disaster, causing spectacular crashes and pileups.

Ramp to Dirt

Moto X can take place on different types of **terrain**. Sand dunes make excellent jumps and give soft landings. Pavement is level and fast. Wooden ramps are often used for long jumps. The most common material used in moto X courses is dirt. It can be raked to smooth the course and piled to make jumps and landings. Dirt is soft, so when riders crash, they will have more protection from injury. Dirt landing ramps are safer because they can be made very large and do not break when a rider lands a record-breaking jump. Most record-breaking daredevils begin their ride on a wooden ramp and land on a dirt ramp. Wooden ramp to wooden ramp is considered more dangerous because the wooden ramp can break.

Centers of Attention

Many big moto X events, such as the X Games, are held in huge stadiums. These events attract sellout crowds of thousands of screaming fans. These are some of the biggest stadiums ever used for moto X events.

Home Depot Center
Carson, CA – 27,000 seats
Wachovia Center –
Philadelphia, PA – 20,444 seats
Staples Center –
Los Angeles, CA – 19,000 seats

In The Money

BIG BUSINESS

Motocross has become a popular sport in North America and around the world. Events are hosted by large companies that want to attract attention to their products. Companies such as Mountain Dew, Taco Bell, and Nike are well-known X Games sponsors. Sponsorship companies pay for the event. In exchange, their name and logo appear in ads for the event, as well as on signs at the event. Advertising helps draw attention to their products. Companies also sponsor moto X athletes. Riders wear company logos on their equipment and **promote** the companies in ads or interviews. Robbie Maddison's New Year's events have been sponsored by Red Bull. As a rider, "Maddo" is sponsored by Red Bull, Swatch, DC Shoes, Yamaha, and many other companies that pay him to ride and break records.

Spending at the Game

On average, how much do people spend at a moto X event?
Ticket: $20
Hot dog: $3.50
Soft drink: $4
Hat: $15
Program: $5

Moneycross

Some athletes earn a living riding moto X. However, they must win events in order to get paid. Moto X is dangerous, and the competitions are challenging. Very few people are able to make a living at moto X, but some have done very well. Ricky Carmichael is the richest moto X rider in history. As one of his sponsors, Honda has paid Carmichael $2 million per year. Each of Carmichaels' other sponsors have also paid him large amounts of money. The best moto X athletes in the world can make more than $5 million per year.

Culture

Extreme Tastes

The most successful moto X riders often have extreme tastes. They risk their lives performing and competing to break records and entertain fans. Punk rock, heavy metal, and hip hop are popular types of music with moto X riders. The best motocross riders have suffered broken backs, legs, and arms. They return to the sport because they love riding.

Fan Support

Record breakers, such as Ricky Carmichael, Travis Pastrana, Ronnie Renner, Robbie Maddison, Jolene Van Vugt, and Ashley Fiolek, have made moto X a hugely popular sport. They have inspired kids, teens, and adults by performing seemingly impossible stunts. Tens of thousands of fans around the world gather at events to watch these moto X stars perform. Many more watch on TV.

QUIZ

1 Who was the first woman to land a backflip?

2 What trick did Travis Pastrana land at the X Games in 2006?

3 Who holds the record for the longest backflip?

4 Who was the first amputee to win an X Games gold medal?

5 What is the name of the X Games moto X high jump contest?

6 What were the first moto X events called?

7 What event is known as "The Race to the Clouds"?

8 Who is known as the G.O.A.T?

9 How do moto X athletes make money?

10 What is Robbie Maddison's nickname?

ANSWERS: 1. Jolene Van Vugt 2. Double backflip 3. Mike Metzger 4. Chris Ridgway 5. Step Up 6. Scrambles 7. The Pikes Peak International Hill Climb 8. Ricky Carmichael 9. Sponsorships 10. Maddo

Glossary

amputated: when a limb is cut off

Arc de Triomphe: a monument in Paris that has been duplicated in Las Vegas

endurance: having enough energy to perform an act for a long period of time

freestyle: a moto x trick competition

gears: parts of an engine that control different speeds

off-road: rough terrain

promote: organizing and bringing attention to an event

prosthetic: an artificial limb

quarter pipe: a type of ramp that sends the rider straight up in the air

suspension: parts of a vehicle that absorb shock from bumps and jumps

table tops: jumps with a flat section on top that joins the takeoff with the landing

tandem: when two riders share a bike

terrain: the ground

whiplash: an injury caused by the jerking of the neck

whoops: a series of small bumps in a stretch of track

X Games: a prestigious extreme sports competition

Index

Log on to www.av2books.com

AV² by Weigl brings you media enhanced books that support active learning. Go to **www.av2books.com**, and enter the special code inside the front cover of this book. You will gain access to enriched and enhanced content that supplements and complements this book. Content includes video, audio, web links, quizzes, a slide show, and activities.

Audio
Listen to sections of the book read aloud.

Video
Watch informative video clips.

Web Link
Find research sites and play interactive games.

Try This!
Complete activities and hands-on experiments.

WHAT'S ONLINE?

Try This! Complete activities and hands-on experiments.	**Web Link** Find research sites and play interactive games.	**Video** Watch informative video clips.	**EXTRA FEATURES**
Pages 10-11 Try this moto X activity.	**Pages 6-7** Learn more about moto X record breakers.	**Pages 4-5** Watch a video about moto X.	**Audio** Hear introductory audio at the top of every page.
Pages 12-13 Test your knowledge of moto X gear.	**Pages 8-9** Read about moto X athletes.	**Pages 14-15** View stars of the sport in action.	**Key Words** Study vocabulary, and play a matching word game.
Pages 16-17 Complete this mapping activity.	**Pages 18-19** Find out more about where moto X events take place.	**Pages 20-21** See moto X athletes on their bikes.	**Slide Show** View images and captions, and try a writing activity.
			AV² Quiz Take this quiz to test your knowledge